YOUR WEALTH

START NOW, START SMALL, KEEP IT SIMPLE

I am neither a reader nor a writer.
I enjoy math, art, and nature.
My loved ones are paramount.

I am a licensed architect.
I am not a financial planner.
I am not a financial advisor.
In fact, I hold no financial certification at all!!!

My wife and I have created wealth for our family.
Additionally, we have created multigenerational wealth.
We have done this without using a financial planner or advisor.

This guide can help you create wealth for your family.
Start now, start small, keep it simple.

YOUR WEALTH

START NOW, START SMALL, KEEP IT SIMPLE

You only need to get rich once.
If you are wealthy, this presentation is not for you.

J. SHEFFIELD

Published by Best Seller Publishing®, St. Augustine, FL
Best Seller Publishing® is a registered trademark.
Printed in the United States of America.

ISBN: 978-1-966395-39-3

For more information, please write:
Best Seller Publishing®
1775 US-1 #1070
St. Augustine, FL 32084
or call 1 (626) 765-9750
Visit us online at: www.BestSellerPublishing.org

Disclaimer

The information provided in this book is for educational purposes only. While the author has made every effort to ensure the accuracy of the information, this book is not intended to be a reader's sole source of financial advice. Readers are encouraged to seek professional consultation for advice specific to their individual circumstances. The author assumes no responsibility for errors or omissions, or for any damages that result from the use of the information contained herein. The publisher and the author make no guarantee of financial results obtained by using this book.

Please note: *Financial decisions have tax consequences. Readers are strongly advised to consult with a qualified tax professional regarding any tax-related matters. The author is not a tax expert and is unable to provide tax advice or guidance.*

All of the tables in this book are readily available on public platforms like Yahoo! Finance and Calculator.net. I encourage you to make use of these readily-available websites for your own use.

All numbers, returns, and data were updated through 12/31/24, unless noted otherwise.

Contents

Introduction

When I was a Boy Scout in my early teens, one of the required Scouting merit badges was Personal Management. This merit badge covered all the essential components of a successful life as well as the fundamentals of wealth creation. First, you had to research potential careers (so you would have money to invest). Second, you learned the concept of compound interest/compound growth (growth rate). Finally, you learned about how the value of your investment increases over time (time invested). These are the three primary components of wealth creation.

$ invested x growth rate x time = wealth

Knowing this equation set me on a path to investing success. Of course, there is more to consider than those three things alone such as choice of investment and commensurate growth rates, which I will speak about later in this book—particularly the importance of the choice of your investment. In the meantime, start contemplating this mantra:

Winners tend to keep winning.

This is one of the major focuses of my simple system. Here is another thing to keep in mind from now on to maximize future wealth:

Take as much risk as you can tolerate for as long as possible.

The greater the risk, the greater the return. Later, we will discuss techniques to identify and estimate "risk/reward," figure out "how much you can tolerate," and examine "value creation over time."

My first Generational Wealth Creation plan started during junior high. I worked to save money for college, and I prepared for college as well as I could by getting decent grades, choosing an economical college to attend, and deciding to pursue a well-paying career.

Once my professional career began, my investing began as well. I maximized my contributions to my 401(k) (employer-sponsored retirement plan) and set up an IRA (individual retirement account). As my income rose, so did my investment contributions. Taxable accounts were set up. Fortunately, I married a like-minded young professional, and through our combined efforts, our wealth plan started to take shape.

I'm an architect, so planning is a natural process for me. Although I started planning for wealth creation while I was young, you don't have to start as a teen or young adult to produce great results for your future. Also, rather than becoming more complex over time, my plan has become simpler and more effective. I continue to simplify our existing assets and focus our additional purchases on a small group of winners, a method that has worked out very well.

This book offers three strategies that, when combined, provide a straightforward plan that can scale to enormous wealth with minimal research, little maintenance, and moderate effort. I encourage you to create your own wealth plan; until you do, though, please consider using the template described in the book.

Inveniam viam aut faciam.
I shall find a way or make one.

I want to point out that wealth creation does not require superior intelligence. I believe rigorous discipline surrounding a simple plan is of greater value than detailed analysis and sophistication.

A simple plan is what you are going to find here. This book is intended to be accessible, actionable, durable, and complete. The plan and the tools I reference can evolve and scale over decades and generations. I believe this book can provide the skills and confidence to create living wealth for you and your family. It references specific information sources to monitor the constant value movement of your investments as well as online resources for calculations and research activities.

If you are intimidated about taking that first step—start now, start small, and keep it simple. As your confidence grows, your wealth will follow.

"Everything should be made as
simple as possible but not simpler."

—Albert Einstein

Master These Two Techniques

To help identify winners, I use a simple chart technique to compare stocks and exchange traded funds (ETFs). You will see examples of these charts throughout the book. The primary purpose of following this method is that the charts automatically indicate both historical and up-to-the-minute information.

I strongly recommend that you take a few minutes to emulate these charts on a computer.

1. Search QQQ Stock (Nasdaq 100 ETF)[1]
2. Pick "Yahoo Finance"
3. Pick "Advanced Chart" (upper right)
4. Pick "5 YR" (lower left)
5. Pick "Comparison" (upper left)
6. Add "MSFT" (Microsoft)
7. Pick "Corporate Events" (upper left)
8. Pick "Dividends" (top of drop-down list)

---

[1] An exchange traded fund containing the 100 largest Nasdaq listed stocks, weighted by market capitalization.

9. The flags along the bottom are the dividend payments
10. Hover over a flag to see the payment amount ...

Try different features and explore the information.

Examples:

I have found that if a stock I'm interested in buying does not keep up with QQQ, I should buy more QQQ instead.

If a stock I'm interested in buying does not keep up with AAPL (Apple), I will buy more AAPL instead.

If a retail stock I'm interested in buying does not keep up with COST (Costco), I will buy COST instead.

Winners tend to keep winning.

CALCULATE COMPOUND GROWTH OVER TIME

This is the primary planning tool to estimate the greatness of compound growth and thus future value.

I strongly recommend that you take a few minutes to emulate these calculations on a computer.

1. Search "Future Value Calculator"
2. Pick "Calculator.net"
3. Number of Periods (N) – plug in the number of years
   a) if quarters, divide the interest rate"by 4
   b) if months, divide the interest rate by 12
4. Starting Amount (PV) – plug in the current amount invested (PV, present value)
5. Interest Rate (I/Y) – plug in the growth rate (I/Y, interest/yield rate per year)

6. Periodic Deposit (PMT) – plug in the amount you intend to add per period (PMT, periodic deposit/ payment)
7. Calculate, BOOM!

Notes:

Be sure to appreciate the total interest, aka growth versus the amount invested.

Try different growth rates and time periods.

Examples:

Start with $1,000 and add $1,000 / year for 20 years at 16% growth rate	=	$153,301
If you let it ride for 10 years without adding money at 16% growth rate	=	$676,277
If you let it ride for 10 more years with-out adding money at 16% growth rate	=	$2,983,352
Keep in mind the total investment	=	$20,000

If you invest $ 1,000 at birth for a child, 16% interest, at 60 years old = $7,370,201

Is 16% growth rate reasonable?

1. It depends on choice of asset
2. Recent history is an estimate!

Annual Return	5 year %	10 year %
QQQ	20.76	17.96
XLK	22.68	20.12
SOXX	23.80	22.75
SPY	15.68	13.25

"Compound interest (growth) is
the eighth wonder of the world."
—Albert Einstein

“The greatest risk is not
taking any risk ...”
—Mark Zuckerberg

Lessons Learned

Starting in 2010, I began to reorganize and ramp up our family assets. I decided to focus primarily on stocks. I was reluctant to add Microsoft, even though it was and still is one of the most valuable companies in the world. The primary reason for that hesitation was the negative sentiment of the investment community, who used cute damnations like "the law of large numbers" and "it's had a good run" to dismiss the sheer greatness of Microsoft's achievements. However, I knew that for decades Microsoft had relentlessly built a behemoth company. So, in the spring of 2017, in spite of the constant hectoring of the investing geniuses, I bought Microsoft stock at $62 per share with my fingers crossed.

1
Strategy 1 — Action Now!

If you do not have a mobile device, get one or borrow one from a trusted individual.

1. Open a Robinhood or SoFi brokerage account and put $25 in it ASAP.

   Because:

   - Fractional share purchases are offered; therefore, we can buy S&P 500 companies in $1 increments.
   - Robinhood and SoFi have superior technological platforms.
   - Mobile app, low fees, banking, and investing—you can scale into your wealth.

1a. What type of brokerage account?

   If you're investing for retirement or education expenses:

   - Open a Traditional IRA or Roth IRA (review Investopedia to determine whether a Traditional IRA or Roth IRA is best for you).

- Open an individual brokerage account, if you prefer unrestricted use of your accumulated wealth. Why not both?

2. Pick 5 of the 20 largest US stocks listed in table 1.

   Why these?

   - Winners tend to keep winning. The huge market capitalization is proof of winning.
   - Phenomenal "scale" to distribute new products and services, and pivot to new opportunities.
   - Superior financial position, access to capital, dividends and share repurchase, low risk of bankruptcy.

3. Buy $5 of each of the 3 that are the most down from their 52-week high.

   Why do this? Because:

   - We always want to buy at a discount.
   - The price is the sum total of all past information; it does not indicate the future.
   - These companies have reached hundreds of all-time highs; they will achieve hundreds more.

4. Congratulations! You have put 3 of the best companies in the world to work for you!

   - Plan to accumulate more of these winners for decades.
   - Monitor but do not obsess. Focus on your work and family.

- Reinvest all dividends. This is a standard feature of your stock account; use it!

5. You have created a personal wealth machine that can scale over years.

   What should you do next?

   - Add $25 per week to your Money Machine following step 3.
   - Every month add another winner until you reach 5 stocks.
   - Do not let any 1 stock get too large compared to the others.

This is the stock segment of your wealth plan.

These are the other segments:

- Chapter 5: ETFs
- Chapter 6: Cash as a hedge
- Chapter 9: Moon Shot (optional)

NOTE: terms and ideas will be discussed later.
Action now!

Strategy 1 **Table 1**

Largest US Companies by Market Capitalization (MC)

2. Pick 5, but no more than 2 from a sector.

	Stock	MC	Sector
1.	AAPL	3.79 T	Behemoth
2.	NVDA	3.29 T	Semiconductor
3.	MSFT	3.13 T	Behemoth
4.	GOOGL	2.33 T	Behemoth
5.	AMZN	2.31 T	Behemoth
6.	META	1.48 T	Media/Adv.
7.	TSLA	1.30 T	Manufacturing
8.	AVGO	1.09 T	Semiconductor
9.	BRK.b	978 B	Money
10.	WMT	726 B	Retail
11.	LLY	695 B	Health
12.	JPM	675 B	Money
13.	V	612 B	Money
14.	MA	484 B	Money
15.	XOM	473 B	Energy
16.	UNH	466 B	Health
17.	ORCL	466 B	Tech
18.	COST	407 B	Retail
19.	PG	395 B	Health
20.	HD	387 B	Retail

Benchmark ETFs:

QQQ	100 largest Nasdaq listed stocks
S&P 500	500 largest US listed stocks

Strategy 1 **Table 1**

Largest US Companies by Market Capitalization (MC)

2. Pick 5, but no more than 2 from a sector.

	Stock	(%) 1 yr. Rtn.	(%) 5 yr. Rtn.	(%) 10 yr. Rtn.
1.	AAPL	35	236	830
2.	NVDA	179	2,139	27,965
3.	MSFT	14	167	812
4.	GOOGL	37	171	649
5.	AMZN	46	130	1,370
6.	META	69	175	669
7.	TSLA	63	1,191	2,772
8.	AVGO	114	642	2,245
9.	BRK.b	25	101	205
10.	WMT	70	133	206
11.	LLY	30	483	1,016
12.	JPM	39	76	306
13.	V	22	68	385
14.	MA	25	76	526
15.	XOM	5	53	19
16.	UNH	-6	75	407
17.	ORCL	60	208	286
18.	COST	41	214	535
19.	PG	13	37	86
20.	HD	13	78	273
Benchmark ETFs:				
	QQQ	27	137	404
	S&P 500	24	82	190

Using Calculator.net, if we invest $25 per week ($1,300 per year) for the next 30 years at a 16% compound annual growth rate:

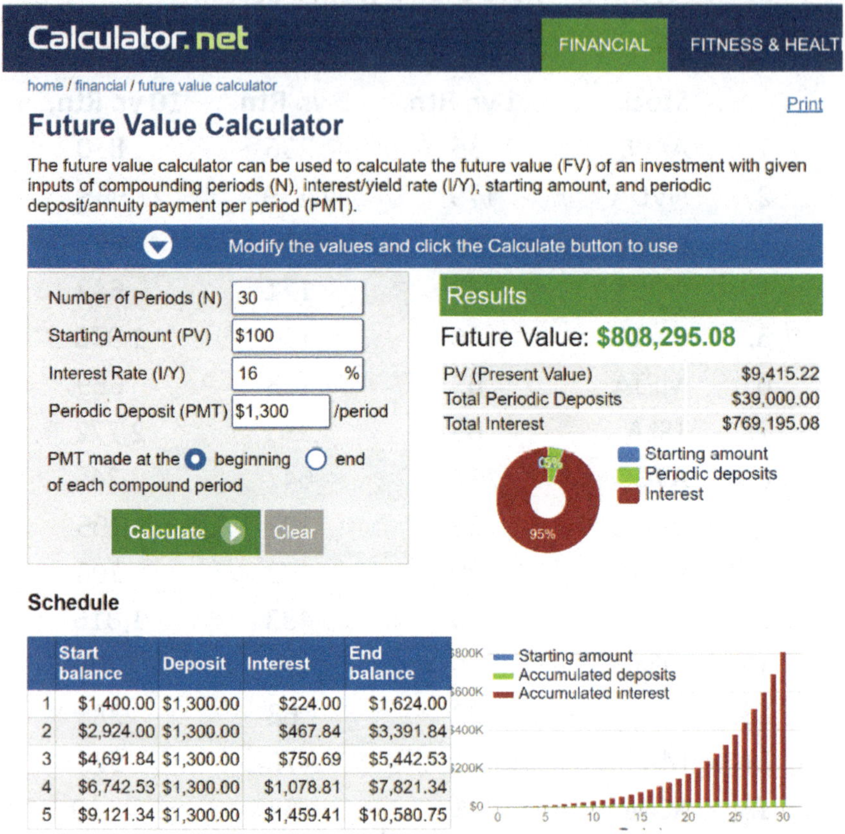
Calculator.net FINANCIAL FITNESS & HEALT

home / financial / future value calculator

Print

Future Value Calculator

The future value calculator can be used to calculate the future value (FV) of an investment with given inputs of compounding periods (N), interest/yield rate (I/Y), starting amount, and periodic deposit/annuity payment per period (PMT).

Modify the values and click the Calculate button to use

Number of Periods (N) 30

Starting Amount (PV) $100

Interest Rate (I/Y) 16 %

Periodic Deposit (PMT) $1,300 /period

PMT made at the beginning end of each compound period

Calculate Clear

Results

Future Value: $808,295.08

PV (Present Value)	$9,415.22
Total Periodic Deposits	$39,000.00
Total Interest	$769,195.08

Starting amount
Periodic deposits
Interest
95%

Schedule

	Start balance	Deposit	Interest	End balance
1	$1,400.00	$1,300.00	$224.00	$1,624.00
2	$2,924.00	$1,300.00	$467.84	$3,391.84
3	$4,691.84	$1,300.00	$750.69	$5,442.53
4	$6,742.53	$1,300.00	$1,078.81	$7,821.34
5	$9,121.34	$1,300.00	$1,459.41	$10,580.75

Note: weekly investment will produce higher returns than yearly calculations shown.

There are no guarantees. We are simply increasing our odds of success:

- Buying proven 5-year and 10-year historical winners

- Buying at a discount to 52-week highs
- Limiting our diversification to sectors with proven 5- and 10-year historical growth

Using Calculator.net, if we invest $100 per week ($5,200 per year) for the next 30 years at a 16% compound annual growth rate:

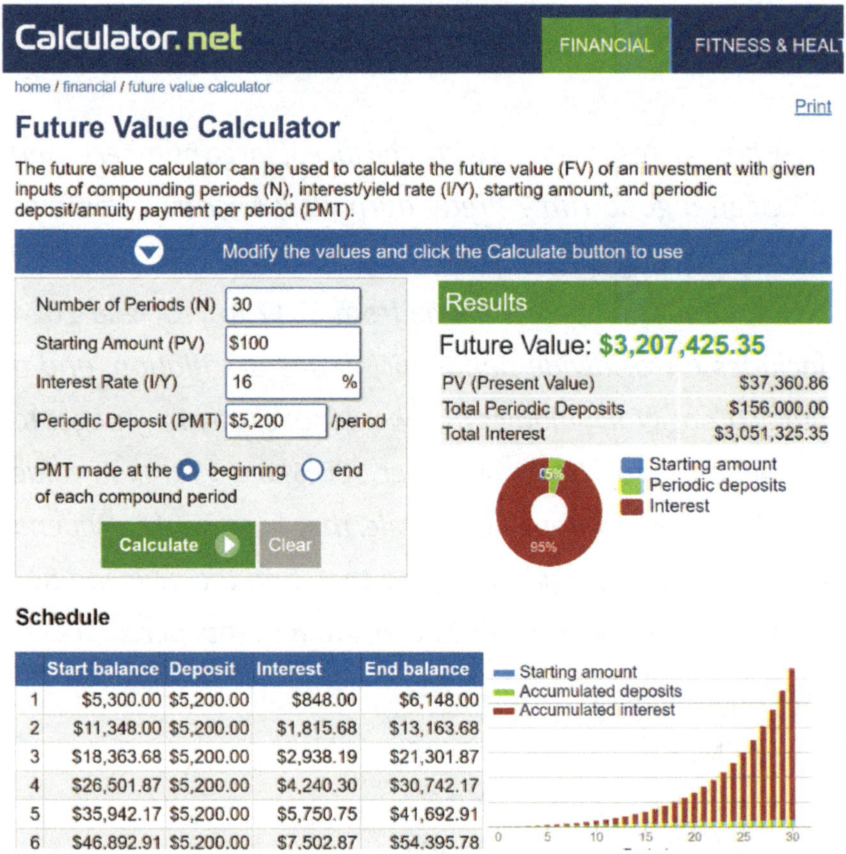

	Start balance	Deposit	Interest	End balance
1	$5,300.00	$5,200.00	$848.00	$6,148.00
2	$11,348.00	$5,200.00	$1,815.68	$13,163.68
3	$18,363.68	$5,200.00	$2,938.19	$21,301.87
4	$26,501.87	$5,200.00	$4,240.30	$30,742.17
5	$35,942.17	$5,200.00	$5,750.75	$41,692.91
6	$46,892.91	$5,200.00	$7,502.87	$54,395.78

Note: weekly investment will produce higher returns than yearly calculations shown.

***Congratulations!* You have taken a giant step toward Your Wealth.**

While your account is being approved:

- Read on then return to Strategy 1 to complete the tasks
- Accumulate cash to fund your stock purchases
- Consider helping a loved one get started

How has Microsoft coped with "the law of large numbers" and "it's been a good run"? Pretty darn well; Microsoft remains one of the largest companies in the world, and the good run continues. The time frame from 2017 to year-end 2024 includes a worldwide pandemic, issues of inflation, and a litany of societal maladies that would take too many pages to list, yet Microsoft has grown over 500% to a $3 trillion value (market capitalization). Meanwhile, they have paid a dividend every quarter, through thick and thin, and the dividend has increased every year from 39 cents to 83 cents per share.

Scoreboard since 3/2017:

MSFT	+561%
QQQ	+259%
S&P 500	+139%
Geniuses	#*&@!

“Compound interest (growth) is
the eighth wonder of the world.”

—Albert Einstein

Lessons Learned

When I was eight years old, my family moved from a farm in Pennsylvania to a farm in Arkansas. The farm had rolling hills, creeks, forested areas, and an old farmhouse. My parents promptly bought a Hereford bull and several Angus cows. The first calves were born, and my parents offered to sell one to me for $5. Fortunately, I accepted, and I named my calf Topsie. As I watched our crops grow from seed, a box of chicks become a flock of egg-laying chickens, and the handful of livestock increase into a herd, the power of compound growth in nature was obvious.

2
Compound Growth

Compound growth refers to the growth of the original entity plus growth of the growth itself. Compound growth can be determined several ways.

The compound growth formula is:

$$Growth\ rate = \left(\frac{Ending\ value}{Original\ value}\right)^{\frac{1}{number\ of\ periods}} - 1$$

Calculator.net is an excellent online resource to calculate compound growth. Future value tables also work well and can help us empirically understand the power of compound growth. Future value tables are also excellent for calculating annuities, which are a stream of payments over time.

To help me fundamentally comprehend the sheer power of compound growth, I like to consider trees. Given some time, soil, water, and sunshine, a pine cone or acorn can become a sapling, then a tree. That tree can multiply and create an entire forest, and each unit of time allows the entire ecosystem to grow simultaneously. The results are phenomenal.

Some tree species grow faster and some slower; some are weak and some are hardy; some need more light, water, spacing, and so on. When I was a teenager in southeastern Oklahoma, I watched the forestry companies clear-cut enormous areas of forest, then immediately plant pine saplings. Within a few years, the forest would begin to recover in earnest, and after a decade, it would be difficult to find the affected areas.

Compound growth calculations can help to manage huge societal issues such as population growth, pension liabilities, civic systems, infrastructure requirements, and so on. Entire countries utilize compound growth to varying degrees of success. For example, Norway created the world's largest sovereign wealth fund by investing a large proportion of the gross domestic surplus into solid compound growth investments: namely, well-established global company stock, aka equities. These investments grow faster than the civic needs, and the virtuous cycle continues, accommodating education, healthcare, pensions, and enormous sovereign wealth.

On a personal level, we can use Norway's example to create our own path to wealth. Using compound growth calculations, we can estimate the amount we need to invest to accommodate future expenses and retirement.

For example, if we begin investing for a child's college education at their birth, the future value of 16% return for 20 years is 19.461. Therefore:

Invested now	x (FV, 16%, 20yrs)	= Amount in 20 years
$ 5,138	x 19.4	= $100,000

Then try different growth rates to determine a comfortable level to invest. Or, we can determine an amount to save per year to reach the goal.

Yrly. Inv. x (FVA, 16%, 20yrs) = Amount in 20 years

$ 870 x 115.380 = $100,000

We can do similar calculations for retirement; future-value annuity at 12% for 40 years is 767.091. Therefore:

Yrly. Inv. x (FVA, 12%, 40yrs) = Amount in 20 years

$ 1,303 x 767.091 = $1,000,000

While enduring the tune of negativity and woe (similar to now and always), I conducted these types of calculations for my family decades ago. We have blown through my highest permutations. GET ON IT!

$$$ invested x growth rate x time = wealth

Compound growth rates are measurements of value creation over time. The faster growth rates belong to entities that can scale their products and services with minimal negative inertia. For example, if a company develops a piece of software, once that product is completed and viable, the company can proliferate the product without a large cost. Contrast this with a manufacturer that produces airplanes. Airplanes are extremely difficult to scale relative to software.

To further evaluate the example above, consider the effect of interest rates. Airplanes are large and require factories, intricate design, extreme safety and regulatory prowess, lots of skilled labor, and above all, time to build. Planes are also very difficult to update. Alternatively, software is small, easy to duplicate, easy to update, and easy to deliver.

You get the idea. For the airplane manufacturer, all these complicated component parts cost money, and interest rates apply to all forms of debt. Thus their compound growth rates vary a lot!

Commodities are raw materials. The issues with commodities and commodity producers are similar to those of the airplane manufacturer. However, the airplane manufacturer has one huge advantage over the commodity producer. The airplane manufacturer can build a superior product that can command a premium price. If a company can maintain a premium product status, the company will put up superior financial performance and the investors will reward the company by buying and holding the stock. But commodities are economically sensitive and tend to be trades rather than investments.

Personally, I favor companies that can scale with ease, have minimal to manageable debt, and a track record of compound growth rates higher than QQQ. If not, I would prefer to simply accumulate more QQQ.

A great advantage of stock and ETF (exchange traded fund) investing is that vast amounts of information are available for the stock or ETF you are considering. The most important consideration to me is the relative historical performance/compound growth rate of the stock or ETF compared to QQQ. As noted, if it cannot keep up with the QQQ, why would I buy it?

To achieve superior results, we want to maintain a reasonable compound growth rate for as long as possible. A key consideration is accumulating assets that provide recurring growth as opposed to one-time payoffs. This may seem obvious; however, I implore you to consider the massive advantages of compound growth over time.

1 2 4 8 16 32 64 128...

The **law of 72** is a handy mathematical device. When you divide 72 by the growth rate, the product gives you the number of years required for an investment to double. For example:

A 10% compound annual growth rate: 72/10% = 7.2 years to double.

A 16% compound annual growth rate: 72/16% = 4.5 years to double.

A 18% compound annual growth rate: 72/18% = 4.0 years to double.

In the next chapter, we will consider the recent historical growth rates of various stocks and ETFs. Since historical stock and ETF performance can be easily found, we can make reasonable projections of future performance. However, we know by now that there are no guarantees; instead, we want to plan and act to increase our odds of success, limit our downside, and take action when a winner becomes a laggard. The key is to stick to winners because winners tend to keep winning.

10 YEAR GROWTH—QQQ, GOLD, ENERGY, BONDS

Chart Notes:

Compound growth is the product of value creation over time. If a product or service can be used to create recurring value for the consumer, a virtuous cycle can occur where profits are increased for both the producer and the consumer. Over time, new products are developed and a multi-year growth trajectory is established: for example, technology (QQQ) used by businesses as a tool for increased productivity.

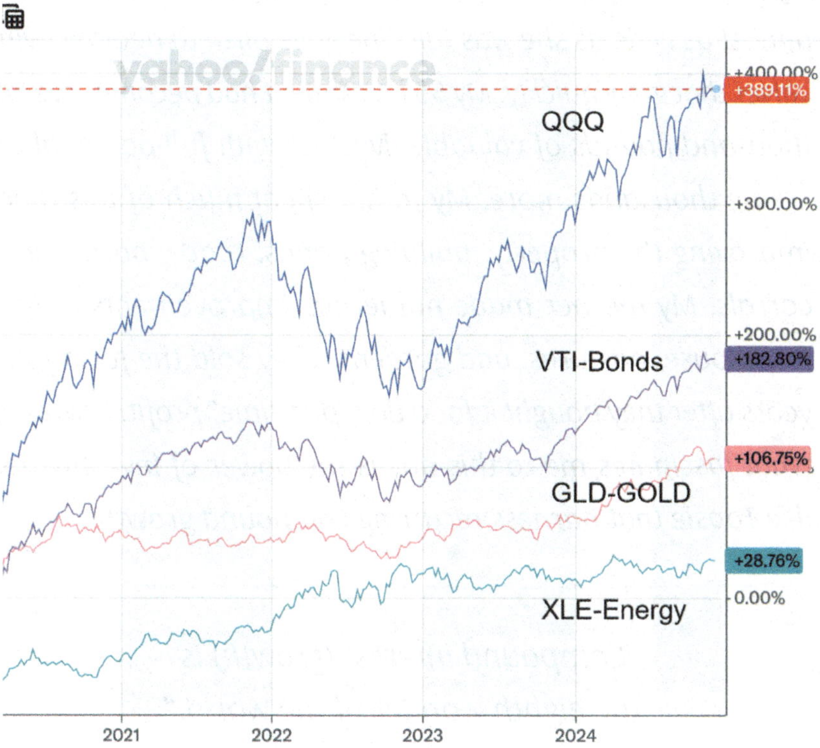

Compound growth is limited for commodity producers due to several factors, including production costs, environmental constraints, one-time benefit, and depletion. Some value is created; however, the compound growth rates are limited and subject to massive cyclical swings.

Back on the farm in Arkansas, a couple of years went by, and my calf Topsie had become a healthy pregnant cow that was almost as wide as she was tall. She gave birth to healthy twin calves that grew quickly. My $5 investment had become several thousand pounds of valuable livestock with full potential to create thousands more. My father spent much of this time improving the property, building ponds, roads, barns, and corrals. My mother made numerous improvements to the farmhouse, pastures, and gardens. They sold the farm four years after they bought it for a tidy "one-time" profit. However, what fascinates me to this day is the power of investments like Topsie that harness recurring compound growth.

> *"Compound interest (growth) is*
> *the eighth wonder of the world."*
> —Albert Einstein

"Winners tend to keep winning."

—The Bull

Lessons Learned

When my son was eight, I asked him if there was a stock he would like for me to buy. He said Amazon. Amazon seemed reasonable to me, so I promptly bought shares in March of 2009 at $3.75 per share. The shares doubled, and I happily sold them in September of 2010 for an excellent 100% return at $7.50* per share. When my son arrived home from school, I announced the triumphant achievement, but to my chagrin, he was not happy. The shares currently trade at $219.39*! In short, I was delighted to take a 100% gain in lieu of riding his winner to a 5,750% gain.*

*AMZN stock split 20/1 6-6-2022

3
CAGR – Compound Annual Growth Rate

Compound annual growth rate is one of the most common measurements of financial growth. It is an excellent method for comparing various investments' relative performances over a period of time. The compound annual growth rate formula defines "n" as years, hence "annual." CAGR is a slight modification to the growth rate calculation:

$$CAGR = \left(\frac{\textit{Ending value}}{\textit{Original value}}\right)^{\frac{1}{\textit{number of years}}} - 1$$

Calculator.net and tables are handy resources for CAGR calculations and planning.

In my life, I own or have owned bonds, gold, silver, real estate, oil and gas properties, MLPs, REITs, royalty trusts, and other investments. I have found that stocks and ETFs (exchange traded funds) offer numerous advantages over these, including a low cost to acquire, low expenses, readily available historical data, well-regulated markets, ease of tracking, ease of storage, near-flawless dividend reinvestment, virtually no maintenance or upkeep, and ease of selling—whether you plan to trade or hold them for decades.

The largest advantage of stocks and ETFs is the opportunity for relatively consistent compound annual growth rates. I believe that, over time, the efficiency of high-quality stocks and ETFs is unmatched. For this and many other reasons, the remainder of this book will focus on stocks (common equities) and ETFs.

The essential elements of wealth creation are invested capital, compound growth rate, and time.

$$$ invested x growth rate x time = wealth

Compound annual growth rate is the measurement of value creation over time. There are various asset types you can choose from to buy for your wealth portfolio. The table in this chapter lists the growth rate of several asset types over the past five and ten years.

Compound annual growth rate (CAGR) varies by asset class and over time. We want to look for and choose assets with growth rates over a period of time similar to the time frame of our wealth plan. I suggest that most wealth plans should be based upon a time frame of more than ten years so we can harness the greatness of compounding. Therefore, for stock picking, I typically use the 5-year and 10-year historical growth rates. I place added emphasis on 5-year returns simply because they reflect recent information.

Quick aside: If you are a young person with high earnings, please consider the same principles listed here. The main difference between your situation and that of most people is that average people (like me) accumulate wealth over time. Therefore, we can adapt, adjust, and prepare for our wealth while it accumulates. When you come into a great deal of money over a short period of time, it can be more challenging to maintain a forward-thinking perspective on what to do with your money.

At any age, when a high level of wealth is achieved, the main priority should be to stay rich. Therefore, consider a strategy of ETFs (listed in the ETF section) that can outgrow your spending and set your family up for multigenerational wealth.

For my purposes, I prefer the empirical approach and observe the market cap growth over time. However, if you prefer an academic approach, consider the following (and note that "secular" refers to trends and developments that persist regardless of economic cycles and seasonal activities).

SECULAR GROWTH

I view the technology behemoths as exemplars of secular growth simply due to the massive scale and innovation driving broad product and service offerings. For example, Nvidia, a semiconductor company, has integrated software into their semiconductor products, which should make the company less cyclical and result in continued secular growth. Artificial Intelligence could be a secular growth engine simply because its value is created through efficiency. In other words, if buying a product or service increases production and profitability at a reasonable price, it should be purchased regardless of economic conditions.

SECULAR DECLINE

Industries and sectors that fall out of favor or become obsolete face secular decline. For example, societal change and regulations have resulted in secular decline of the tobacco industry. Innovation and consumer preferences have resulted in secular decline of the pharmacy and media companies. Climate change initiatives have resulted in energy innovations that reduce the reliance on carbon-based oil and gas production. Persistent poor management can lead to a company's secular decline. Regardless of the reasons, we want to avoid companies in secular decline.

CYCLICAL

This refers to the standard economic and business cycle of expansion and contraction of the gross domestic product (GDP). For example, materials stocks are beholden to the economic cycle because the economy needs more input commodities during an economic boom and fewer input commodities during an economic slowdown. Manufacturing and consumer discretionary stocks are also cyclical based upon interest rates and consumer budgeting. I place all companies with non-differentiated products and services in this category.

NONCYCLICAL/NONSECULAR

For my purposes, this is where I place most of healthcare and military-related companies. Most people will not cut spending on critical healthcare products and services for their loved ones. Insurance seems to cover more and more procedures, which also reduces the consumer budgeting aspects of healthcare consumption. Similarly, our national defense is critical regardless of the economic cycle.

Choosing investments with superior compound annual growth rates is the key to wealth creation. In subsequent chapters, we will look at simple techniques I use to identify secular growth companies as well as tactics to avoid slow-growth laggards. The goal is to increase our chances of successful investing by identifying winners, buy them on the dips, and ride the growth for as long as possible.

Winners tend to keep winning.

TABLE 2:

The upper portion of the table lists several ETFs' yearly performance for the past ten years with the negative years highlighted. VOO is the Vanguard S&P 500 ETF that tracks the performance of the 500 largest US companies weighted by market cap.

Table 2

Selected ETF returns by year

	% VOO	% QQQ	% XLK	% SOXX
2024	24.15	26.99	24.05	16.41
2023	10.58	54.85	56.02	67.00
2022	-18.15	-32.49	-27.71	-35.04
2021	28.66	27.57	34.55	44.00
2020	18.25	48.60	43.67	52.93
2019	31.29	39.12	49.97	62.37
2018	-4.45	-0.14	-1.56	-6.47
2017	21.69	32.70	34.27	39.83
2016	11.80	7.01	14.81	38.41
2015	1.34	9.54	5.62	-2.06
10 Yr. Rtn.	190	404	474	619
Annual Rtn.	13.31	17.96	20.12	22.75

VOO	Vanguard S&P 500 ETF
QQQ	Nasdaq 100 ETF
XLK	Technology Sector Spyder ETF
SOXX	Semiconductor Index ETF

Table 2

Selected ETF return by year

	% GLD	% BND	% USO	% TQQQ
2024	26.99	-1.82	14.87	64.41
2023	12.69	5.66	-4.94	226.98
2022	-.77	-13.11	28.97	-86.00
2021	-4.15	-1.86	64.68	119.00
2020	24.81	7.71	-67.79	70.03
2019	17.86	8.84	32.61	229.84
2018	-1.94	-.11	-19.57	-38.94
2017	12.81	3.57	2.47	141.55
2016	8.03	2.53	6.55	113.38
2015	-10.67	.56	-45.97	-20.72
10 Yr. Rtn.	108	-14	-49	1,963
Annual Rtn.	7.97	1.52	-9.88	34.16

GLD Gold ETF
BND Vanguard Total Bond Market Index ETF
USO Oil ETF
TQQQ 3 times the QQQ performance (up or down) ETF

TABLE 3:

As previously noted, the S&P 500 is an index composed of the 500 hundred largest US companies according to market capitalization. Further, SPGI categorizes the 500 companies into 11 sectors listed here.

Table 3:

S&P 500 Index – Sector Weighting and Historical Returns

ETF Ticker	Sector	Current Weight %	Historical Returns 1 Yr. %	5 Yr. %	10 Yr. %
XLK	Technology	32.63	22	157	474
XLF	Financials	13.44	28	57	147
XLY	Consumer Discretionary	10.91	26	80	217
XLV	Health Care	10.58	1	35	98
XLC	Communication Services	8.88	34	81	92
XLI	Industrials	7.69	16	62	140
XLP	Consumer Staples	5.69	9	25	61
XLE	Energy	3.44	1	42	14
XLU	Utilities	2.64	20	18	60
XLRE	Real Estate	2.24	1	5	35
XLB	Materials	1.85	-2	37	77
SPY	S&P 500	100.00	24	83	190
QQQ	Nasdaq 100	~	27	137	404

One component has dragged the group higher over the past five years (and started to take over years before that). SPGI is the sector spyder[2] administrator. SPGI has made an attempt to keep other sectors relevant by placing TSLA, META, AMZN, and GOOGL in other sectors and not in the technology sector ETF.

---

2 Spyders are products of SPGI. Spyders are ETFs that focus on each of the 11 S&P 500 sectors. For example, XLK is the technology sector spyder.

Regarding the Amazon family dissention noted at the beginning of the chapter, the good news is that I bought a much larger amount of Amazon in January of 2011 at $8.40. At the current price of around $219.39, our gain is around 2,512%. Compound growth is indeed magical; the doubling effect can be ginormous given time.*

Scoreboard since 3/2009:

AMZN	+5,750%
QQQ	+1,586%
Dad	&*#@!%

* AMZN stock split 20/1 6-6-2022

"Software is eating the world, but
AI is going to eat software."

— Jensen Huang

Lessons Learned

About the time I retired from architecture in 2017, I decided to buy one last high-end graphics computer. I asked my then 15-year-old Son to come along and help me choose. We drove over to Best Buy and he led me directly to the most expensive notebook computer. I said, "Why is it so expensive?" He pointed at the Nvidia sticker and walked off to the gaming area. Within a minute or so a salesperson came by and said, "Nice choice." I asked, "Why is it so expensive?" He pointed at the Nvidia sticker. On the drive home I realized my mistake and our problem. We owned Intel stock!

4
Market Capitalization Growth

During our wealth plan creation and refinement, I've focused on market capitalization above any other measurement to determine a company's potential to provide superior compound growth. Market capitalization, (Market cap, or MC) is a standard metric that can be found on your iPhone stock app, Yahoo Finance, or calculated with simple math.

market cap = number of shares x the share price

Market cap is especially useful because it's a simple way to measure the size of one company versus any other company. In my view, market cap growth is instructive to stock picking because market cap growth is the sum total of all these metrics plus investors' willingness to buy (or sell) additional shares. The number of shares is fairly constant with the exception of occasional secondary offerings, which increase the number of shares, and the mirror image company buybacks, which reduce the number of shares. Regardless, the share price changes constantly whenever the stock market is open.

Watching market cap growth too closely is unnecessary and a waste of time. However, a quarterly update can help us determine which companies are growing steadily and which companies are declining. Short stints of market cap contraction can be normal; however, year-over-year decline should be addressed.

Accumulate winners and sell the laggards.

Our goal is simple: identify and accumulate winners because they grow. It follows that the companies with the largest market caps have outgrown their competitors and proven the ability to create products and services with sales that are durable through various economic conditions.

As stock owners, we have the opportunity to benefit from our stock in two primary ways: capital appreciation and dividend payments. Occasionally, we may also benefit from a company spin-off; however, they are somewhat unusual and difficult to anticipate. What we can easily do is determine the sectors that outperform. Then look at the top performers in the outperforming sectors. To find these, I review the top ten holdings of the top performing ETFs. Over time and with some practice, you will see that a small group of stocks has powered sector outperformance. You will notice that sector ETFs are heavily concentrated on the MC-20 companies (Chapter 1).

As an example, a decade ago, I decided to buy the ten largest tech stocks in QQQ, which remains my favorite ETF. The QQQ is a weighted index of the 100 largest market cap companies listed on the Nasdaq stock exchange; therefore, it is mostly tech but not entirely. My thought was that over time, I would determine the five winners to keep and sell the five laggards. In some cases, I decided to replace a laggard with a winner.

	Basis	Cap. Apr.	Div. Apr.	Total Apr.
NVDA	100,762	3,429,168	43,991	3,473,159
APPL	100,175	1,223,150	213,898	1,437,048
AVGO	100,341	949,474	200,328	1,149,802
MSFT	100,464	531,861	57,347	589,208
META	100,322	606,945	2,008	608,953

The total return of the group is +1,294%. The CAGR is roughly 30%.

Identify winning companies that grow their market caps, buy the dips, and ride the rips. Winners tend to keep winning.

As noted, the S&P 500 is the 500 largest United States companies weighted by market cap. Within the S&P 500, technology is the clear leader in market cap growth. Over the past 40 years, the technology sector has grown from a few percent of the S&P 500 to well over 30%. Conversely, most other sectors have become a smaller percentage of the S&P 500.

A technique I use to select winners is market cap per employee.

	MC	EEs	MC/EE	10yr rtn (%)
Disney	201B	173,250	1.16M	20
Netflix	381B	13,000	**29.3M**	1,807
Intel	86B	124,100	.693M	-44
Nivida	3,289B	29,600	**111M**	27,965
Citibank	133B	229,000	.581M	38
Visa	612B	28,000	**21.8M**	384
Ford	39B	177,000	.220M	-34
Tesla	1,296B	140,473	**9.2M**	2,772
ATT	163B	143,630	1.13M	-9
Apple	3,785B	164,000	**23.1M**	830

Since market cap growth fuels the growth of our portfolio, it follows that we want to select the most efficient competitors. In my opinion, this metric identifies the companies that utilize technology to provide superior products and services. I favor this simple analysis because it is based on actual current information. In other words, it is not influenced or limited by expert estimates.

To drive performance of our portfolio, I want to take as much risk as I can tolerate for as long as possible. Therefore, market cap growth is the primary focus of my portfolio.

There are two sacrifices I knowingly make in order to drive performance. One sacrifice is maintaining cash equivalents that have little risk and little return. The other sacrifice is diversification.

A diversified portfolio mitigates risk and, therefore, mitigates returns. A diversified portfolio can occasionally outperform a market cap growth portfolio in the short run. However, in the long run, a market cap growth portfolio dominates a diversified portfolio. Since personal expenses are ongoing, cash on hand can cover expenses during times when the portfolio is down, thus protecting the long-run winners from being sold to cover expenses.

The technology sector has become so large that the products and services are increasingly more diversified. For example, Amazon includes retail, web services, advertising, entertainment, artificial intelligence, logistics, and any other market Amazon chooses to enter.

Over time, I want to buy the dips and ride the rips. To buy the dips, I need to believe that the company will figure out the problem, take action, and emerge stronger than ever. For my purposes, the companies with superior market cap growth provide that confidence.

In my opinion, the technology sector is best positioned to provide profitable growth via artificial intelligence. Jensen Huang has stated: "It is clear that AI is going to impact every industry." I trust Mr. Huang over all the expert-geniuses combined.

Quote Lookup
NVIDIA Corporation (NVDA)
NasdaqGS - Nasdaq Real Time Price • USD
134.29 -3.20 (-2.33%)
At close: December 31 at 4:00:01 PM EST
134.29
Comparisons
Indicators
Technicals
Corporate Events
O 44.84 H 47.61 L 44.37 C 45.46 Vol 2.11b
2016
2017
2018
2019
2020

Chart Notes:

	10-year return
NVDA	+26,584%
INTC	-44%

Regarding the Intel dilemma: I bought Intel because, at the time, Intel paid a 5% dividend. However, when I compared INTC and NVDA on a chart, INTC's dividend was respectable but the capital appreciation was pathetic. NVDA's dividend was pathetic, but the capital appreciation was nothing short of phenomenal! Therefore, I sold INTC for a small profit and purchased Nvidia at $3.79 per share.*

Scoreboard since 5/2017:

NVDA	+5,050%
QQQ	+276%
INTC	-44%

*Nvidia did a 4 for 1 split 7-20-2021 and a 10 for 1 split 6-10-2024

Avoid laggards; if you own a laggard, identify it and take action.

"Time is money."

—Benjamin Franklin

Lessons Learned

Blue Chip Growth (BCG) was a popular investment theme for many years. I got complacent and bought several of these (BCG) darlings, specifically Starbucks, Nike, Cisco, Intel, and most unfortunately, Disney, in 2017. I bought Disney for $97 a share. I watched the ups and downs and noticed its underperformance relative to the innovation-rich QQQ. Nevertheless, I decided to stick with Disney and hope for a rigor mortis convulsion, then sell it if the stock got near a high. Alas, hope is not a strategy.

5
Strategy 2 — Exchange Traded Funds (ETFs)

This simple strategy focuses on four ETFs. I highlight these four due to their superior historical compound growth rates. As usual, the higher risk provides the higher return over time.

ETF	5-year	10-year	Market Capitalization Weighted
VOO	15.7%	13.3%	500 largest S&P stocks
QQQ	20.8%	17.9%	100 largest Nasdaq stocks
XLK	22.7%	20.1%	+/-72 technology companies of the S&P 500
SOXX	23.8%	22.7%	+/-30 semiconductor companies

I am not suggesting that you buy all of them. Instead, a simple solution is to determine which ETF fits your risk tolerance and accumulate that one for as long as possible. If the least risk/least reward is too volatile for your preferences, then watch the performance for a while and perhaps you'll become less risk averse through observation.

The chart in this chapter places these ETFs side by side. You can see how each handled COVID-19 and inflation issues. Also reflect on the numerous negative issues and developments that are all incorporated into the growth rates and prices over time.

A common refrain in investing literature is "past performance is no guarantee of future results." Absolutely correct. We should never expect guarantees of any kind. Instead, we are developing a plan to "increase our odds of successful investing." In my view, the value of looking at historical returns is to determine which companies have demonstrated outperformance and most likely could extend that outperformance into the future.

Conversely, does it make sense to buy a proven laggard hoping they become a winner? Regarding ETFs, you can use the "winners tend to keep winning" mantra in these two ways:

1. Determine and buy ETFs that outperform.
2. Since ETFs are weighted by market capitalization and adjusted accordingly over time, the ETF will automatically adjust to a higher concentration of the winners and gradually eliminate the laggards. As my son says, these ETFs utilize "good old-fashioned AI" to stay ahead of the game.

Referring to the MC-20, the 20 largest market capitalization companies, currently the VOO contains all 20: QQQ 9, XLK 5, SOXX 2. This is a useful datum to monitor market capitalization changes over time.

You may find a dilemma inherent to this strategy is that there does not appear to be an investing platform that offers ETF fractional shares; at least, I have not found one. As indicated on the chart, all of these ETFs cost $200+ per share/unit. However, I think it is worthwhile to save up and buy these rather than settle for an inferior, low-share-price ETF. The primary reason is that as long as you can tolerate the dips, these ETFs can be owned for many years. Taxes are not due until you take the gain (if any), so the capital appreciation is tax deferred until you sell. Be aware that dividend income is taxed in the current year. Refer to Investopedia.com and your tax service for tax information.

Another consideration and benefit of these ETFs are extremely low fees and expenses. These ETFs efficiently and at a low cost provide the service of amalgamating dozens of stocks and adjusting for market capitalization, which is extremely valuable.

Tactically, if we plan to accumulate ETFs for many years, we can implement one of several simple methods of accumulation. We can simply buy at routine times, aka, dollar-cost averaging. This is typically how 401(k) contributions work.

What I prefer to do is look at the chart and determine a "price channel" (refer to Chapter 7). Then I wait for the price to hit or get near the lower line of the channel. We can do simple math to determine what percentage drop from the high is represented by the line and buy at that price point. If I am traveling or focused on other things, I set a "limit buy order" at my price. The purchase will automatically occur if the stock drops to that level. This calculated approach removes most of the emotion from the trade.

Keep in mind, these dips and rips occur due to three primary components:

1. How the companies are performing
2. How the sector is performing
3. General sentiment (mood) of the investor group

With regard to proven winners in growth sectors, all three of these factors are short-term. Our wealth is created over the long-term. Therefore, we can use these dips opportunistically to buy winners at a discount. Additionally, we can accumulate cash when the ETF rips higher to deploy on the subsequent dips.

If this sounds complicated, you can simply dollar-cost average into winners and let time pass while the companies adjust to the short-term maladies. Keep in mind that all these problems have led to winners reaching hundreds of subsequent all-time highs.

The following is a hypothetical comparison of the four ETFs based upon the 10-year historical returns. If we bought $5,000 per year worth of each ETF at the beginning of each year for 30 years:

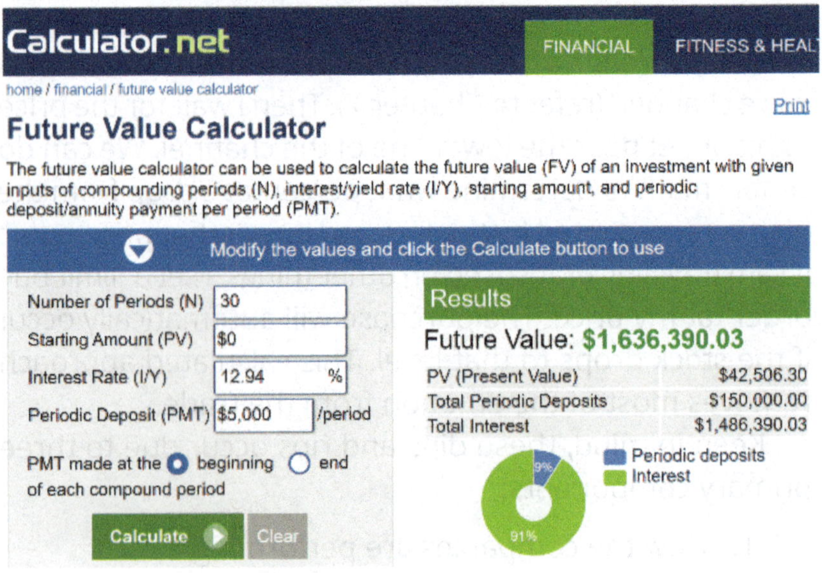

VOO $1,636,390

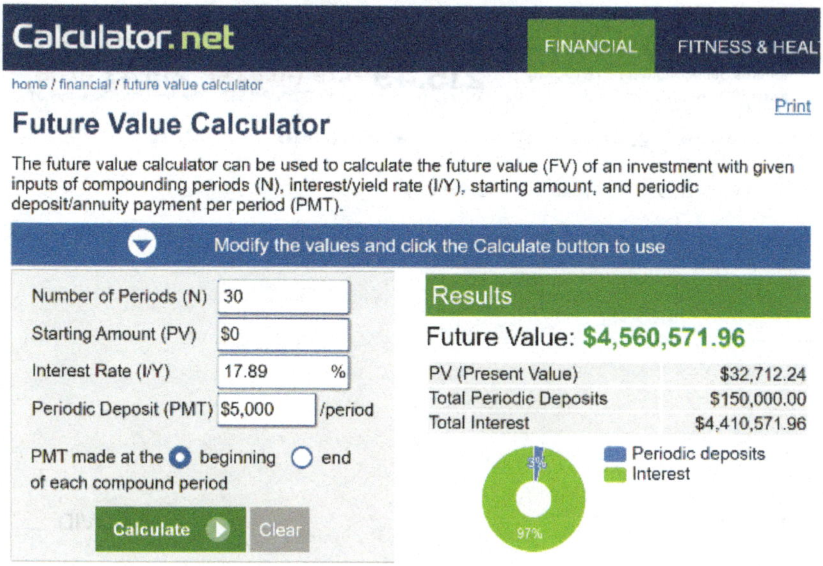

QQQ $4,560,571

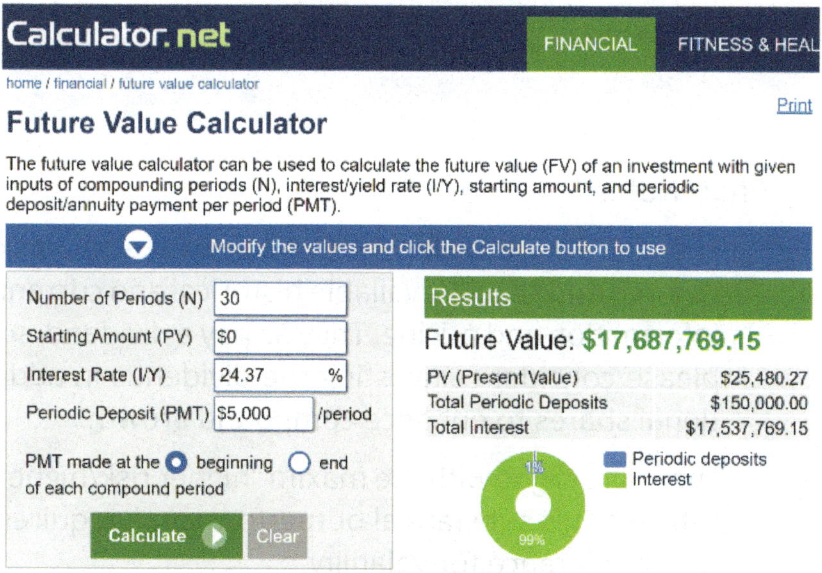

SOXX $17,687,769

(not shown) XLK $7,211,080

Chart Notes:

> These ETFs are widely held with long-term track records and readily available historical and current information and pricing. They all pay a dividend, so please consider reinvesting the dividends in additional shares to enhance compound growth.
>
> The chart aligns with the maxim "higher risk/higher return." This substantial outperformance requires a high tolerance for volatility.

If we anticipate volatility, we can buy the commensurate dips and enhance our long-term return. The resulting lower basis reduces our risk of losses and increases our chances of successful investing.

The sum total of all historical events—both good and terrible—are incorporated in the price. Each of these ETFs have reached dozens of all-time highs in the past year.

Disney did have a last-gasp move higher, and I sold it at $130 on the way up to the all-time high of $203 in 2021 (sadly, that remains the all-time high). Fortunately, I bought QQQ with the proceeds. Since then, Disney is -19% while QQQ has marched higher by +76%. Had I simply bought QQQ in 2017, the return would be +228% while Disney is +3%.

Over time, Starbucks, Nike, Cisco, Intel, and Disney have all been purged from my portfolio due to lackluster gains, and the proceeds have been consolidated into QQQ. Better late than never.

If a stock has not kept up with the five- and ten-year returns of QQQ, why would I buy or keep it?

Scoreboard since 2014:

DIS	+3%
QQQ	+228%
S&P 500	+120%

"All things being equal, the simplest
solution tends to be the best one."
—William of Ockham

Lesson Learned

During the fall of 2017, I decided to accumulate PayPal stock. My basis was $66, and I was confident that PayPal would do well alongside my traditional bank stock JP Morgan. Still, I watched for a dip that would trigger my -20% (below my basis) because that equals hard sell. Instead, PayPal moved higher in a series of higher-highs to a crescendo of $296 in early summer of 2021. I felt like a hero but did not want to sell and pay the long-term capital gains tax. After all, PayPal was reinventing banking in the bold new cashless society, right?

6
Master Plan

Most investors and financial professionals refer to the collection of your individual assets as your "portfolio." Works for me; however, I call our portfolio "Mule." Regardless, the idea is an organizational construct that helps us plan and track accumulated assets, asset value, performance, growth, and income over time.

> **Invested $$$**: This is the cumulative of one-time asset purchases plus annuity purchases (the stream of purchases over time).
>
> **x**
>
> **CAGR** (choice of assets): This is the primary focus of several chapters of this book.
>
> **x**
>
> **Time** (time frame): For purposes of this project, five years is the minimum I would consider. We seldom see market-wide sell-offs that last more than five years from previous highs, to sell off low, to fresh highs again. **However, in the short-term, those declines can be brutal and very difficult to endure without selling.**
>
> **=**

Wealth (purpose): Typically, the objective is to fund retirement, educational expense, and so on. My purpose is independence.

If five years seems to you to be a reasonable amount of time and you can tolerate the volatility (not sell during a dip), then I suggest you consider the 5-year and 10-year CAGR as a reasonable guide.

There are no guarantees; we simply strive to improve our odds of successful investing.

If you agree, then plan out a reasonable amount to invest per week or month. Set up a spreadsheet with reasonable parameters and make a list of assets to accumulate.

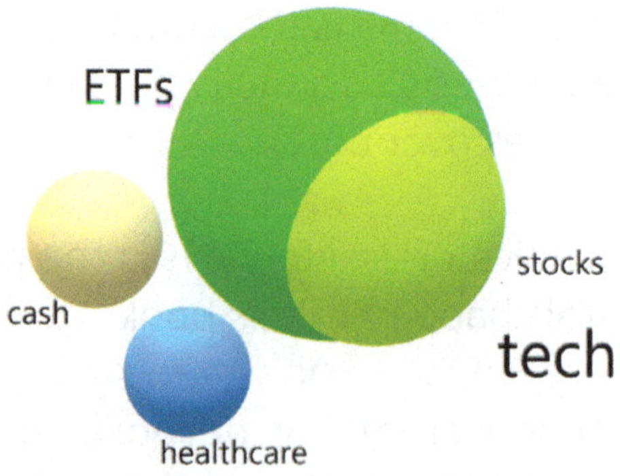

Diagram of Mule components.

The Tech component includes ETFs and stocks.

As you implement Chapter 1, MC-20 stocks, you are building out a primary component of your portfolio. You can choose stocks that you believe will provide compound growth and offer some stability through various market conditions. I have found that healthcare tends to do well when technology is lagging and vice versa. Therefore, the diagram roughly emulates our portfolio: lots of technology, plenty of healthcare, and plenty of cash.

I'm comfortable with this heavy technology focus because I believe growth is far more important than income, and I believe technology will continue to provide superior profitable growth. Additionally, I'm not concerned about the occasional, short-term contraction of the total asset value since I keep a large amount of cash as a hedge to protect the growth assets from being sold during a downturn in technology. Most importantly, there have been countless reasons to sell stocks and ETFs, yet the overall market hit numerous all-time highs during the course of 2024.

In my opinion, creating a simple master plan requires a small number of components. You want just enough parts to allow you to harness growth, hedge downturns, and most importantly, result in your wealth creation.

The simplest plan has three components:

1. assets that grow faster than the overall economy (secular growth)
2. assets that grow regardless of the economic conditions (noncyclical)
3. cash

With that in mind, consider the composition of the Mule portfolio. Mule is heavily weighted toward technology (secular growth), with the balance equally weighted with healthcare (noncyclical) and cash.

The relative sizes (amount of value in each) should be based upon your tolerance for risk. The relative values and the overall values will change daily. I suggest you consider tracking the extreme high values (52-week highs) and the extreme low values (52-week lows) to reduce the stress of daily fluctuations. It's fair to focus on the extreme highs so long as we remain in control of "when" we sell. Never lose sight of the fact that the market goes up over time.

Buy the dips, ride the rips.

In order to buy the dips, we need to have cash on hand. A simple technique is to accumulate cash during market highs to deploy during sell-offs. Over time, buying at a discount should increase the returns. However, since quality winners tend to go up over time, dollar-cost averaging (aka routine purchases) can also produce excellent results.

The healthcare component of Mule is entirely stocks and no ETFs. The reason is that there are too many laggard healthcare companies and, in my view, only a small group of winners. This is why I haven't found a healthcare ETF that I'm willing to buy.

Instead of buying ETFs, ten years ago, I bought a meaningful dollar amount of ten proven healthcare winners. Over the years, I sold the laggards and kept the winners. Currently, I own four healthcare stocks: UNH, LLY, TMO and ABBV. As noted, the healthcare stocks tend to do well when technology is weak and vice versa. This provides the hedge I strive for. I strategically bought technology when it was weak and healthcare was strong. Keep in mind, the media and experts are mostly short-term focused. Our master plan should be long-term focused.

	Basis	Cap. Apr.	Div. Apr.	Total Apr.
LLY	100,098	1,295,528	386,201	1,681,729
ABBV	100,125	261,495	187,619	494,114
UNH	100,060	529,230	109,343	638,573
TMO	100,072	193,867	5,304	199,171

These companies were winners long before I bought them.

The cash portion of the portfolio is vital to the master plan. Cash provides peace of mind, cash prevents the sale of stocks and ETFs during market dips, and cash allows us to buy those dips. I have observed, and the experts generally agree, that the market tends to sell off in the spring and fall. Conversely, the market tends to run up in the summer and winter. Accumulating and deploying cash in opposition to the market seasonality has been a great way to accumulate winners at a discount.

I saved cash from zero. In other words, one week worth of income, then one month, then one year. Available cash allows Mule to be heavily weighted to growth for as long as possible.

Mule is NOT diversified. Instead, I intentionally built a portfolio that I believe will harness compound growth for decades. Therefore, I am taking as much risk as I can tolerate for as long as possible.

Chart Notes:

Ten-year chart of select Mule components.

Three of four components of Mule are represented on the chart.

		10-year return
Chapter 1/ Strategy 1.	MC-20 — LLY	+1,015%
Chapter 5/ Strategy 2.	ETF — QQQ	+404%
Chapter 9/ Strategy 3.	Moon Shot — TQQQ	+1,963%

Cash is not shown on the chart; however, I use a Vanguard money market mutual fund (VMRXX) to accumulate and store cash.

From mid-2021 to mid-2022, PayPal stock took a nasty dive from the $290s to the $60s, and my tax problem was solved the environmental science way—it evaporated. As I watched, I figured that PayPal would recognize the problem, take action, and at least stabilize near a previous low. Instead, like a hot knife through butter, PayPal sliced lower toward my basis. I finally sold in November of 2022 at $73 for a whopping 10% gain. Had I sold 10% off the top, I could have paid the tax and still had a 227% profit.

Scoreboard since fall of 2017:

PYPL	+31%
JPM	+153%
QQQ	+254%

If a winner turns into a laggard, sell it, pay the tax (if any), and redeploy to a winner.

"The tops are the riskiest times to invest; near the lows are the safest."

—jS (not pictured)

Lessons Learned

In 2016, I decided to buy Walgreens stock; it's the consistent, 108-year-old dividend aristocrat. So, I waited for a dip then purchased it in May of 2016 for $75 per share. The stock (WAG re-tickered WBA) hung in there for a year or so, paying a nice dividend and a respectable capital appreciation well into the $80s per share. So, all is well with the steady-eddy dividend aristocrat, right?

My wager: -20% (below the basis) equals hard sell!

7
Volatility and Charts

There are three primary points to consider regarding volatility. First, volatility is necessary, routine, and constantly occurring. Second, volatility allows us to buy the highest quality growth investments at a discount. Third, time and discipline allow us to ride the volatility to harness powerful long-term compound growth.

Volatility is the turbulence created by price discovery. In other words, buyers and sellers are constantly setting the price of stocks and ETFs. If the price gets too high, the sellers sell. If the price gets too low, the buyers buy. It is a normal routine and a constant process.

All stocks and ETFs are volatile; how volatile depends largely on growth or lack of growth. The primary reason I own stocks and ETFs is growth. A stock or ETF's growth rate, and a plethora of other metrics, are constantly being evaluated and estimated by experts. The short-term bias of the experts provides a fantastic opportunity for long-term investors to buy the highest quality stocks at a discount.

Here is a simple technique I use: (1) decide what I want to buy; (2) wait for two down days in a row; (3) if the third day is lower, I buy, especially if the investment is down in morning trade. What invariably happens is that the sellers eventually get exhausted and buyers step in to take advantage of the discounted share price.

Over time, the cumulative effect of volatility pushes quality stocks and ETFs appreciably higher. In order to benefit from the long-term compound growth, we need to ride through the routine volatility. Charts are empirical tools we can use to help us make volatility a beneficial aspect of our successful trading and wealth creation.

Charts are visual indicators of volatility, and there are dozens of useful chart formations. I will focus on four chart formations that I typically use. With these chart formations, we can identify winners, accumulate winners on the dips, identify and avoid buying laggards, and methodically eliminate past winners that begin to lag.

Most charts indicate the stock price over time. The stock price is the amalgamation of all information regarding the company: financial, gossip, fear-mongering, pie-eyed optimism, FED speak, hand-wringing, saber-rattling, scary bears, friendly bulls, dire prophecies, ALL OF IT! The excellent news is the price line of quality companies and ETFs (winners) move higher over time. The move upward in quality stocks and ETFs is due to additive value creation, regardless of the litany of negative blather. The virtuous multi-decade cycle of wealth creation forms a **higher highs/higher lows** chart pattern.

Comparing two or more stocks on the same chart is a great way to identify winners and laggards. Once we establish a winner, we can draw a price "channel" on a multi-year chart.

To create the price channel, draw a line that connects the high points, then draw a parallel line that connects the low points. Ignore the two or three extreme highs, and ignore the two or three extreme lows. The resulting "channel" will extend into the future. The space between the lines is the trading range over time. When the stock we want to buy is near the top of the range, the smart move is to accumulate cash in order to buy when the stock is trading near the lower line. In other words: Buy Low!

Every few years, the price channel/trading range is disrupted. For example, during the COVID-19 pandemic, the companies that allowed society to work and learn remotely went much higher, creating a parabolic trading range. Simultaneously, travel and in-person entertainment moved lower. These anomalies are exaggerated by short-term buyers and sellers.

Multi-year upward price channels are composed of numerous short-term sell-offs. There are three additional chart formations that can help us take advantage of the sell-off to buy quality stocks at a discount. These are the most useful formations for me: cup and handle, double top/double bottom, and head and shoulders/inverted head and shoulders.

For our purposes, the negative disruptions (sell-offs) can be anticipated by looking for two chart formations: **double/multiple tops and head and shoulders** patterns. Both patterns can indicate that buyers have become exhausted at a high price before the stock can set a new higher/high. Both patterns can be an indication of a short-term sell-off. Keep in mind, all investors want to sell high to lock in a profit. However, when we lock in short-term gains, we may sacrifice overwhelming long-term gains. Think NVDA!

Regardless of why or when a sell-off begins, the sell-off tends to make a **cup formation**, a pattern literally shaped like a cup. A cup formation indicates a stock or ETF that has moved higher in a series of higher highs forming the left portion of the chart. Then, for any number of reasons, the stock or ETF becomes "overbought," setting up for a double top or a head and shoulders formation. During the sell-off, the price grinds lower, making a series of lower/lows until the stock or ETF hits a bottom. The bottom is frequently not obvious; however, a double bottom or inverted head and shoulders typically forms. The bottom is created by the sellers becoming exhausted and the buyers taking advantage of the discount. When the bottom holds and the stock or ETF begins to "recover," it goes on to make a series of higher highs relative to the bottom.

Once the stock or ETF has bottomed, the price channel becomes a guide for accumulating the stock along the lower line of the channel. The handle is the sideways price channel that often follows a cup formation. The handle occurs at the level of the high price prior to the cup. The short-term sideways channel is an equilibrium created by some investors giving up on the stock and others buying in anticipation of the move higher that often follows. Once the sellers are finished, the buyers tend to take quality stocks and ETFs appreciably higher through a series of higher highs/higher lows.

In summary, charts indicate volatility, and we can observe the charts in order to use volatility to confidently make three critical decisions:

> Decision One — If we are buying, we wait for the next pullback and buy at a discount price near or below the lower line of the channel.
>
> Decision Two — When the price is above the channel, we can consider selling to lock in a profit and/or to cover near-term expenses.
>
> Decision Three — If the price drops below the price channel for an extended period of time, we may have a past winner that has become a laggard, and we need to consider selling.

Head and Shoulders

Inverted Head Shoulders

Cup

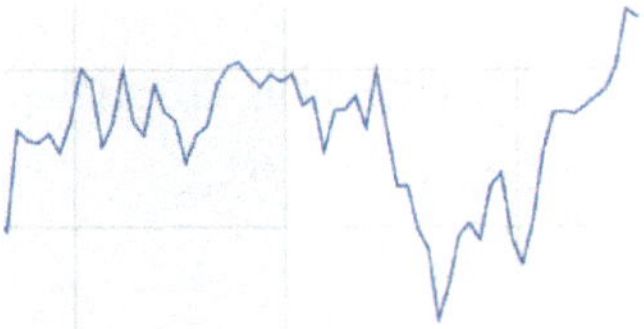

Multiple Tops

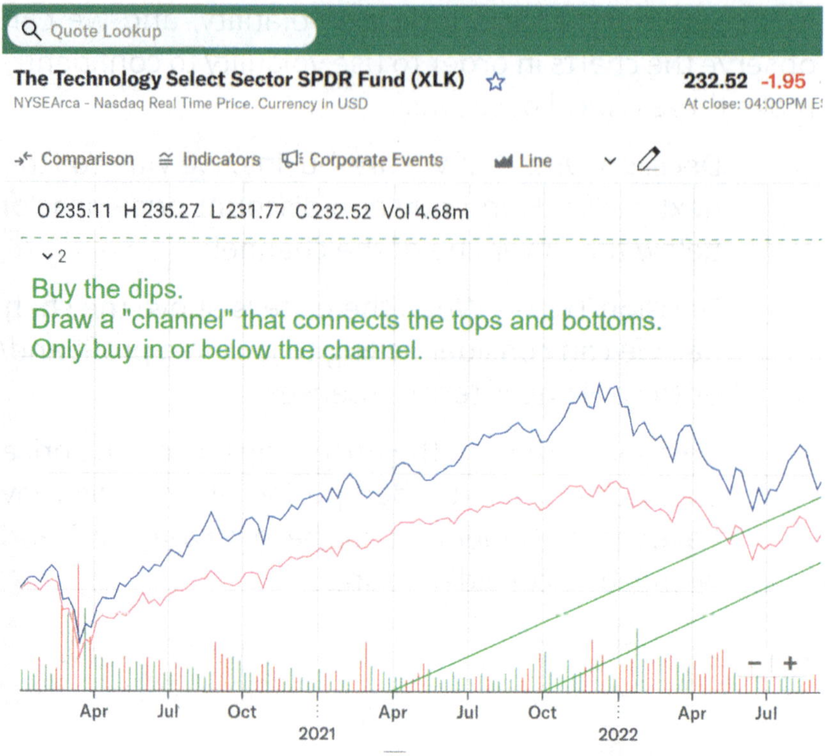

Chart Notes:

The price channel is the space between the green parallel lines.

This chart demonstrates higher highs, higher lows.

The pink line, VOO (S&P 500), falls further behind as time passes.

Notice the double tops that lead to drops, aka, cup formations.

yahoo!finance
(-0.83%)
232.50 -0.02 (-0.01%)
:ST
After hours: 07:55PM EST
+151.81%
+100.00%
+81.82%
+50.00%
0.00%
4.68M
Oct
Apr
Jul
Oct
Apr
Jul
Oct
2023
2024
20

By early 2018, my Walgreens "safe play" thesis was tested. I have a general rule that I live by and think you should consider as well: -20% equals hard sell! No emotion, just sell it and learn from the mistake. In June of 2018, Walgreens dropped to $60 a share, which was -20% of my basis, sell, sell, sell. Since May of 2016, Walgreens is -89%! The primary thought is that I risk 20% for the opportunity of infinite gains. Occasionally I buy a stinker, but I sell it, learn from it, and move on.

Had I simply bought the S&P 500, I'd have earned +187%. From QQQ, my earnings would have been +380%. Please find a percentage you are comfortable wagering and stick to it.

Scoreboard since 2016:

WBA	-88%
QQQ	+380%
S&P 500	+187%

"The market is often stupid, but you can't focus on that. Focus on the underlying value of dividends and earnings."

—John C. (Jack) Bogle

Lessons Learned

A common refrain in the early 2010s was about the aging of the population and its strain on pension funds, Medicare, and society in general. Therefore, I decided to pick a few healthcare stocks to go along with my United Healthcare stock (UNH). I made a simple list of stocks with a high priority on dividend yield, thinking that I could reinvest the dividend payments in additional shares of the stock. Then when the stock took off, all those reinvested shares would take off as well. I reviewed the largest pharmaceutical companies, listed their dividend yield, and considered the consistency of their dividend histories. I noticed that Pharma-Z had paid a consistent dividend for decades. The problem with the stock price was the overwhelming "patent cliff" chorus. One day, someone called into a long-running investing program and asked about Pharma-Z. The host repeated the common refrain: "PATENT CLIFF—DON'T BUY!" So, I bought (Pharma-Z) in 2015 for an average price of $49 per share.

8
Dividends

Total return, aka, total shareholder return or "TSR," is primarily composed of two parts: (1) capital gains (the current asset value minus the basis, or "the amount paid for the asset") and (2) dividends (the optional cash payments made by the company to the shareholder). Although dividends are optional, well-established quality companies have a track record of dividend payments that we can review to increase the odds of our receiving dividend payments that will contribute to total shareholder returns. Oftentimes, you will see the dividend of a company listed as "yield." For example, open the stock app on an iPhone and look at Apple (AAPL). Under the chart, scroll right and look at the top line. It should read "yield." This is the percent of the share price that is paid yearly (in four quarterly payments) via dividend.

Dividend Yield is a simple calculation we can use to compare companies with various stock prices and dividend amounts:

$$\frac{\textbf{Stock price}}{\textbf{Dividends per year}} = \textbf{Dividend yield}$$

As noted, the goal is to accumulate winners. An indicator of a winning stock is a steadily increasing dividend. Typically, companies that choose to pay a dividend pay that dividend quarterly and raise the dividend once a year. Some companies, such as Costco (COST) and CME Group (CME), pay a special dividend based upon strong company performance. Costco occasionally rewards shareholders with a one-time special dividend as well. CME pays a quarterly dividend plus a variable dividend at the end of each year. Special dividends are like manna from heaven; personally, I reinvest all dividends of any kind and hold the shares for as long as possible to harness compound growth.

Strategically speaking, we want to pick companies that routinely increase their dividends. To figure this out, I utilize Yahoo Finance: advanced chart/events/ 5-year and 10-year charts. The flags along the bottom are dividend payments. Hover over them to see the dividend amount paid and review from bottom left to bottom right. This way, we can calculate the percent increase over time and compare companies. An increasing dividend is an excellent indication of company strength and reliability.

Reinvesting the dividend payments in additional shares is an excellent method to harness the power of compound growth. Consider that every time a stock hits an all-time high, the original shares purchased plus all the reinvested dividend payments are hitting all-time highs as well.

Can dividends really make that big of a difference in your financial outlook? My family's wealth portfolio is affectionately called the Mule. After many years of accumulating excellent companies and ETFs, and reinvesting all dividend payments, our Mule yields more in dividends than we spend in a given year. Also, on average, our portfolio components increase their yearly dividend by approximately 5%. This means that we can live on the dividend and allow the portfolio to grow in perpetuity. The Mule is a personal money machine fueled by compound growth and dividends.

Dividends are cash payments; therefore, if the shares are held in a taxable account, the taxes are due in the current year even if we reinvest the dividend in additional shares. Investopedia is an excellent online resource for up-to-date tax information.

To determine whether a stock is paying a reasonable dividend, compare the stocks dividend yield to the dividend yield of the S&P 500 and the QQQ. Ideally, we prefer a company to invest in the profitable growth in lieu of a dividend. However, well-established and high-quality companies can provide capital appreciation and support a healthy increasing dividend. A well-established company will have a track record of dividend increases. We can do simple calculations to determine the percentage of dividend increases. These dividend growers are winners!

We also want to make our best estimate of the companies' commitment to a robust and durable dividend during good times and bad. COVID-19 was a tragedy; however, it was also an excellent financial test for investments.

We can review 10-year charts to identify the companies that increased and maintained their dividend payments through these times and to avoid those that cut their dividend payments.

Quality companies will set dividend payments that are sustainable. Therefore, if the stock price drops, the yield increases. So long as the dividend is maintained we are literally being paid more (a higher dividend yield) to own the stock. As the stock price increases, the dividend yield naturally goes down. However, when the company increases the dividend, the yield increases accordingly.

In practice, I like to buy high-quality stocks (companies) when the majority of experts are selling. I do this because:

1. buying at a discount increases our share count
2. high-quality companies figure it out and return to highs
3. I can increase my dividend yield

Broadcom (AVGO) is an example. I had followed AVGO for some years and was looking for a chance to buy a dip. In the fall of 2018, Broadcom purchased Computer Associates (CA). Most of the experts disliked the acquisition, and the stock price suffered. My confidence was with the AVGO leader, Hock E. Tan. A 10-year chart tells the story of their success. The dividend has increased from $.175 to $.59. The stock price has increased from $22 to $232. I have reinvested all dividends in additional shares and never sold any shares. The reinvested dividends are worth 200% of the original investment, and the capital appreciation is worth 846%. The total shareholder return is currently 1,146%.

In my opinion, the Broadcom example makes three key points:

1. Winners tend to keep winning. Thank you, Mr. Tan!
2. Short-term problems are opportunities to buy winners.
3. Compound growth creates wealth, not short-term blather.

The absolute key is that media and expert noise is inherently short-term.

Wealth creation is based upon long-term compound growth.

Never reach for high yields. These typically mean that the dividend is unsustainable. Look at the COVID-19 pandemic and other challenging financial periods to weed out and avoid weak companies that cut or eliminate their dividend during hard times. Periodically review your stocks to identify companies that are not increasing their dividends commensurate with the winners. If you identify weakness, take action before the company announces a dividend cut.

We want to accumulate companies (stocks) with increasing durable dividends, reinvest all dividends in additional shares, monitor over time, and hold onto winners. Then in retirement, if desired, we have the option of taking the dividends in cash to supplement our retirement income.

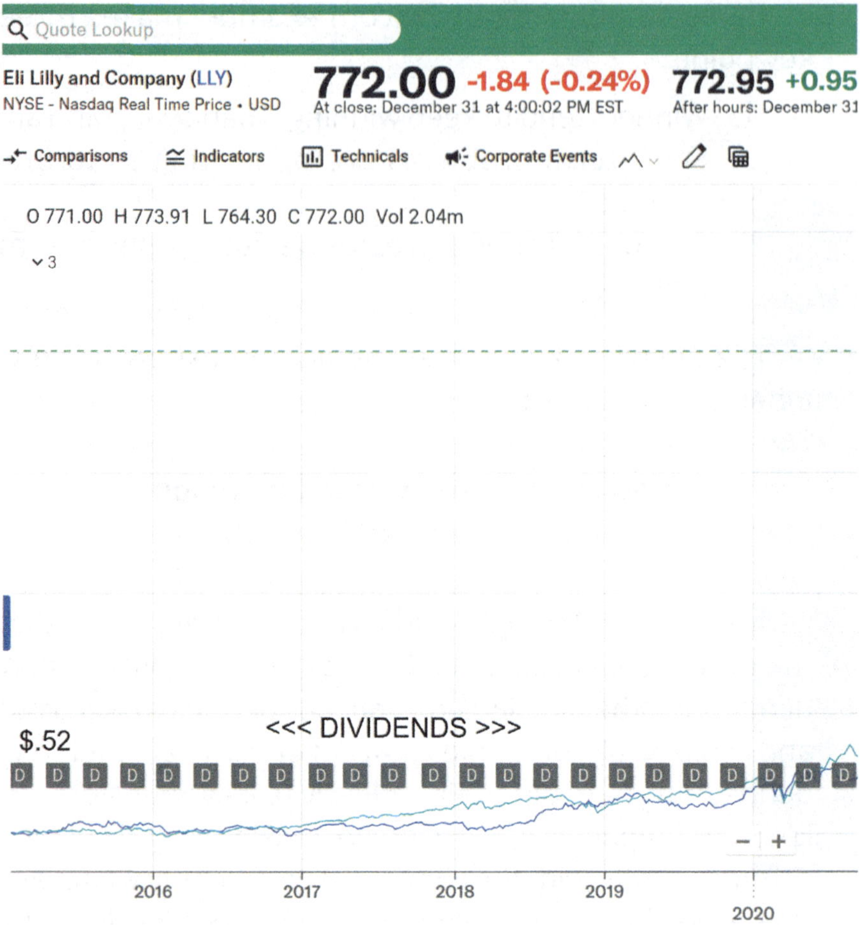

Chart Notes:

Since all dividends have been reinvested in additional shares and the share price has increased, the reinvested dividends are worth 3.86 times the original total cost of the shares.

The reinvested dividends have purchased 499.5 additional shares, which are roughly 23% of the total shareholder return.

The quarterly dividends have increased every year from .50, .51, .52, .53, .563, .645, .74, .85, .98, and 1.13 to 1.30 currently.

The original cost of the shares was $100,098. The total dividend payments we receive are currently $11,966 per year.

Praise be, Pharma-Z (from the beginning of the chapter) is Ely Lilly (LLY). The patent-cliff narrative was an example of the experts repeating the same dross ad nauseam. Eventually, the negativity is priced into the stock. Meanwhile, a great company like LLY fixes the problem and has the opportunity to come out of the funk "gunz-blazin." By 2019, the LLY stock price had moved into the $130s, by 2021 into the $280s, by 2023 into the $500s, and in 2024 into the $800s+. I have diligently reinvested every quarterly dividend in additional shares and kept track of the total shares owned on my spreadsheet. The dividend has steadily increased from 52 cents per share to $1.30 per share. The reinvested dividends are worth 3.86 times the original purchase price of the shares. The capital appreciation is worth 13 times the original purchase price.

Scoreboard since 2015:

LLY	+1,004%
UNH	+376%
QQQ	+398%

"Take as much risk as you can tolerate for as long as possible."

—jS.

Lessons Learned

During the summer of 2018, a friend and I went skiing in South America. The tour company paired us with a family from the Carolinas. On a van ride up the mountain, my friend and I were discussing stocks. The patriarch of the Carolina family overheard our conversation and asked for a marijuana stock to buy. I said to buy Canopy Growth Company (CGC) at $25 and sell it at $50.*

During the trip, we also got to know the man's adult children. My friend and I told them that we accumulate QQQ (Invesco Nasdaq 100 ETF) and the like for the long haul.

---

*CGC 1/10 reverse stock split; meaning, you get one share for every 10 you previously owned. Yikes!

9
Strategy 3 — Moon Shots

These strategies are optional and not necessary to create wealth. However, they have worked for me, so here they are for your consideration. The three ETFs are interchangeable in these strategies.

STRATEGY 3-A. "SIMPLE"

Buy and hold TQQQ. It's that simple. TQQQ is 3 times the daily performance of QQQ up or down. As we know, QQQ is the 100 largest Nasdaq stocks weighted by market capitalization. Therefore, all the superior benefits of QQQ are inherent to TQQQ.

Further, TQQQ has a 5-year growth rate of 33% and a 10-year of 34%. Appling the law of 72, 72/36, TQQQ doubles every 2 years on average. Note, the past 5-year performance includes the impact from COVID-19 and inflation issues as well as several international conflicts.

What is the catch? Volatility! However, if we can manage volatility, we have the opportunity to harness phenomenal compound growth. Additionally, we can use the volatility to buy at a discount during the frequent and severe dips.

$$$ x CAGR x time = wealth

With this notional formula in mind, I decided to conduct a multi-year experiment. I bought a significant amount of TQQQ. However, it was an amount I could afford to lose without disrupting my family's normal life. Additionally, I have the conviction to hold it through thick and thin for decades. No caveats, no capitulation. I did not wait for a dip and simply bought it all at once in August of 2017. Thus far, TQQQ is right on track with its standard overall performance. The gain is currently 725%. However, please review the chart on the following page and take special note of the severe volatility.

STRATEGY 3-B. DOLLAR-COST AVERAGE

Dollar-cost average into TECL. TECL is 3 times the daily performance of XLK up or down. XLK is the technology sector stocks of the S&P 500. Although there are 70+ component stocks, the composition of XLK is weighted heavily toward Microsoft, Apple, and Nvidia. The TECL 5-year growth rate is 34.76% and 10-year is 38.29%.

Consider routinely buying $1,000 of TECL every year for 20 years. If we round down to 38% and plug the information into the Future Value Calculator provided by Calculator.net ... WOW!

A total investment of $20,000 over the next 20 years has a (moon)shot of growing to a value of $2,200,000+.

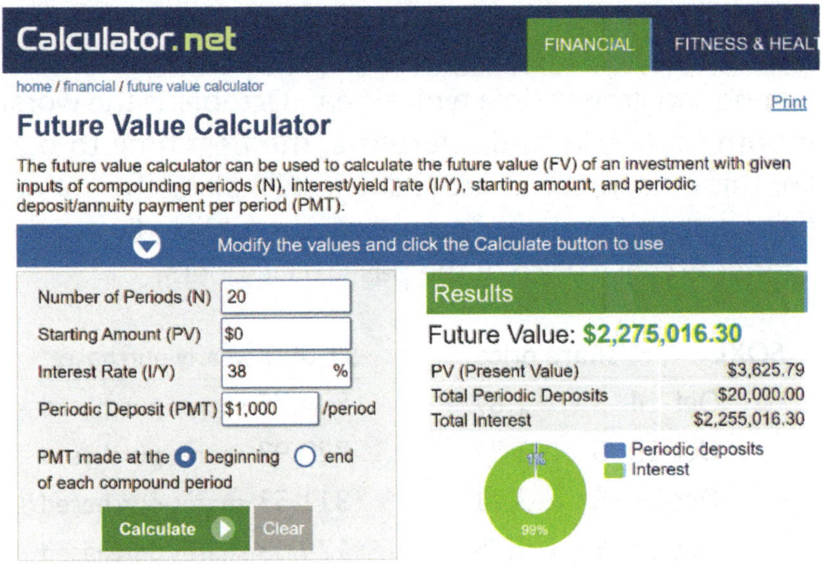

There are no guarantees; this is a simple calculation based upon recent historical returns. Please carefully consider whether you think the risk is commensurate with the reward.

STRATEGY 3-C. DOLLAR-COST AVERAGE—OCTOBER

SOXL is an ETF that is 3 times the daily performance of SOXX up or down. There are roughly 30 component stocks; however, SOXX is heavily weighted toward Nvidia, Broadcom, and AMD. SOXL has a 5-year annual growth rate of 14.31% and a 10-year growth rate of 29.18%. Appling the law of 72, 72/29, SOXL doubles every 2.5 years on average. Note, the past 5 years include COVID-19 and inflation issues.

Similar to the other moon-shot strategies, volatility must be addressed or ignored to harness phenomenal compound growth. In a typical year, October is the worst month for stocks and, therefore, the best time to buy. For this reason, the strategy suggests making the annual purchases in October of each year. The table indicates the share purchase price of the past 10 Octobers.

SOXL		share price		$1,000	yearly purchase
Oct-14	$	1.87		534.76	shares purchased
Oct-15	$	1.37		729.93	shares purchased
Oct-16	$	3.21		311.53	shares purchased
Oct-17	$	7.75		129.03	shares purchased
Oct-18	$	10.39		96.25	shares purchased
Oct-19	$	11.57		86.43	shares purchased
Oct-20	$	17.52		57.08	shares purchased
Oct-21	$	40.50		24.69	shares purchased
Oct-22	$	9.09		110.01	shares purchased
Oct-23	$	18.95		52.77	shares purchased
paid/share	**$**	**4.69**		**2132.47**	**shares owned**
31-Dec	$	27.31	$	58,238	total value
			$	10,000	total paid
gain/share	$	22.62	$	48,236.52	total gain
				382%	**total % gain**

The next three charts show the growth of $5,000 invested for 10 years in each 3x moon-shot ETF.

Is it worth a (moon) shot?

TQQQ	return	$ 5,000	Starting	
2014	1.5682	7,841		
15	1.1741	8,707		
16	1.1104	9,668		
17	2.1865	21,139	Value	
18	0.8035	16,985	by	
19	2.3393	39,733	Year	
20	2.0985	83,380		Can
21	1.8200	151,751		You
22	0.2100	31,868	<<<---	Tolerate
23	2.9826	95,049		This ?
12.31.24	1.6441	**$ 156,270**	**Current Value**	

TECL	return	$ 5,000	Starting	
2014	1.5213	7,607		
15	1.0477	7,969		
16	1.3698	10,916		
17	2.2498	24,560	Value	
18	0.7600	18,665	by	
19	3.0027	56,046	Year	
20	1.6912	94,786		Can
21	2.1300	201,894		You
22	0.2600	52,492	<<<---	Tolerate
23	3.0313	159,120		This ?
12.31.24	1.4700	**$ 233,907**	**Current Value**	

SOXL	return	$ 5,000	Starting	
2014	1.9616	9,808		
15	0.7928	7,776		
16	2.1338	16,592		
17	2.4155	40,078	Value	
18	0.6106	24,472	by	
19	3.2984	80,717	Year	
20	1.7003	137,243		Can
21	2.1900	300,562		You
22	0.1400	42,079	<<<---	Tolerate
23	3.2698	137,589		This ?
12.31.24	0.9740	**$ 134,012**	**Current Value**	

Chart notes:

	10 Year Total Return
TECL	+2,675%
TQQQ	+1,963%
SOXL	+1,242%

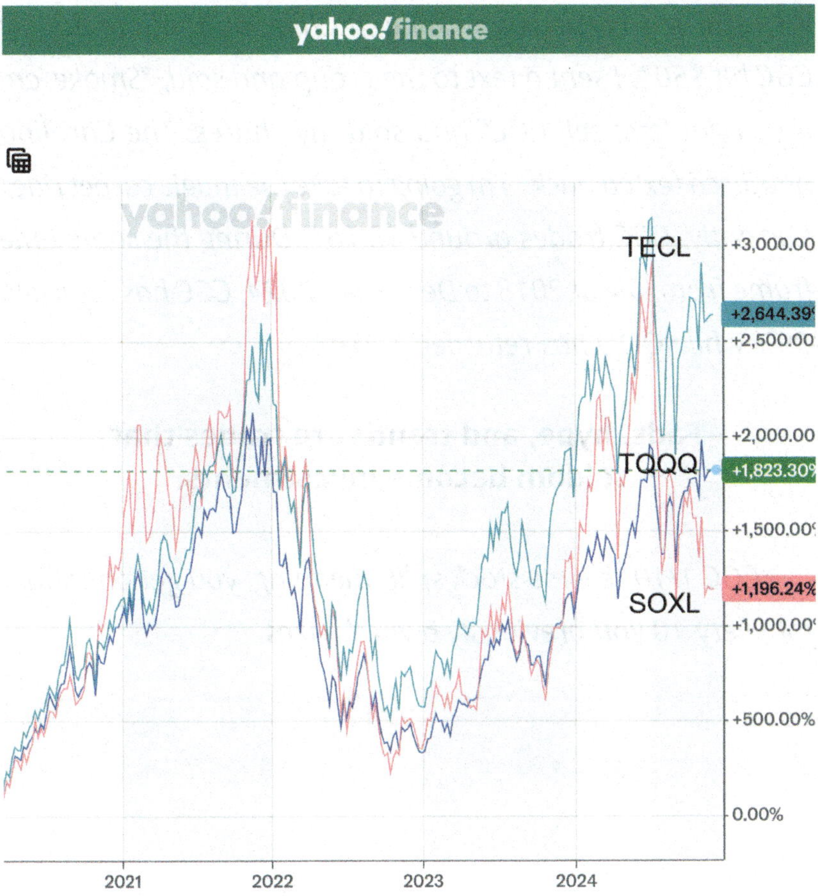

yahoo!finance
TECL
TQQQ
SOXL
+3,000.00
+2,644.39
+2,500.00
+2,000.00
+1,823.30%
+1,500.00
+1,196.24%
+1,000.00
+500.00%
0.00%
2021
2022
2023
2024

We returned home from skiing in Chile, and in late August, CGC hit $50. I sent a text to the group and said, "Smoke 'em if you got 'em; sell CGC" and sold my shares. The Carolina patriarch texted back, "I'm going to take the magic carpet ride." Currently, CGC trades around $2.75*. During the same time frame from July of 2018 to December 2024, CGC has returned -99% while QQQ has returned +201%.*

Fads, hype, and trends are trades that seldom become investments.

**CGC 1/10 reverse stock split; meaning, you get one share for every 10 you previously owned. Yikes.*

Summary and Outlook

Money invested, compound growth, and time are the keys to wealth creation. Quality stocks and ETFs can provide superior compound growth so long as we can tolerate the routine negative swings in value. A simple growth-oriented investment plan applied with rigor has the potential to result in phenomenal wealth.

My hope is that you start now, start small, expect sell-offs and setbacks, develop your simple plan, and persevere to wealth creation. As time goes by, your confidence will most likely grow along with your wealth.

My overarching goal is to help hardworking people with their wealth creation. Moreover, we can help the youth in our lives get started early and find their path to financial independence.

$$ Invested x CAGR x Time = Your Wealth

If I can help further explain or implement those efforts, please contact me. yw25js@gmail.com

As you take on this endeavor, keep top of mind:

1. Winners tend to keep winning. *jS.*
2. Compound interest (growth) is the eighth wonder of the world. *Albert Einstein*
3. Time is money. *Benjamin Franklin*
4. Take as much risk as you can tolerate for as long as possible. *jS.*
5. Buy the dips, ride the rips. *jS.*
6. The dips are the safest time to buy quality. *jS.*
7. No guarantees; we strive to increase our odds of success. *jS.*
8. The greatest risk is not taking any risk. *Mark Zuckerburg*
9. Time is your friend; impulse is your enemy. *Jack Bogle*

Made in the USA
Monee, IL
03 November 2026

67387941R00066